Proud To Be Muslim: The Coloring Book

By Laila Abdulmalik

Dedicated to my daughter, Q'oriankha + my father, Hasan.

This Book Belongs To:

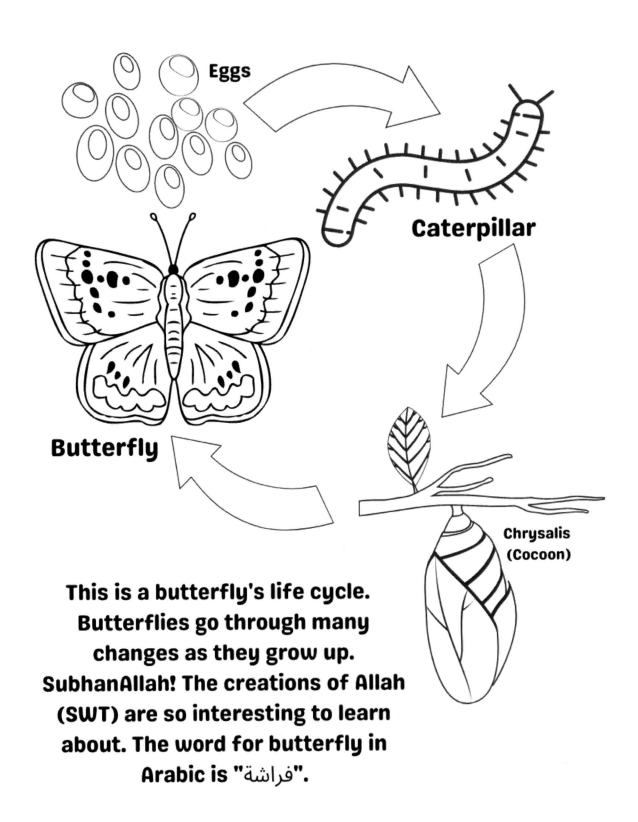

Eggs

Caterpillar

Butterfly

Chrysalis (Cocoon)

This is a butterfly's life cycle. Butterflies go through many changes as they grow up. SubhanAllah! The creations of Allah (SWT) are so interesting to learn about. The word for butterfly in Arabic is "فراشة".

Which do you prefer?

Apple

تفاح

or

Banana

موز

The Five Pillars of Islam

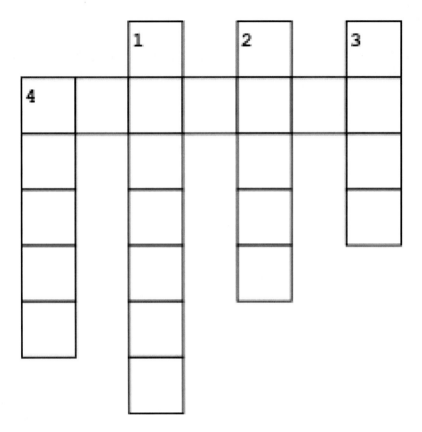

Down

1. No eating or drinking from Fajr until Magrib. We do this everyday during Ramadan.

2. Giving charity to people that need it.

3. Traveling to Mecca for a special religious reason.

4. Something Muslims are required to do five times a day.

Across

4. The declaration of faith that states "There is no God but Allah, and Muhammad is the Messenger of God".

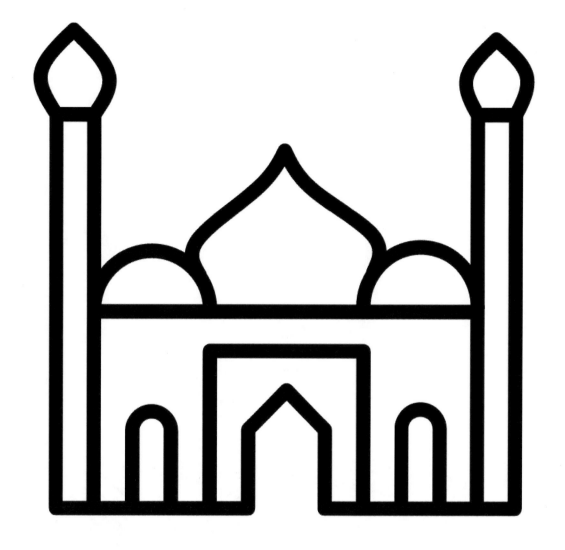

Mosque

Do you like these Halal Foods?

Eggs

Carrot

Ice Cream

What is your favorite color?

To ask someone this in Arabic, you would say:

ما هو لونك المفضل

The Arabic word for horse is "حصان".

DUA

Alhamdulilah for all the beautiful flowers Allah (SWT) has created for us to enjoy!

What is the best Eid gift you've ever gotten?

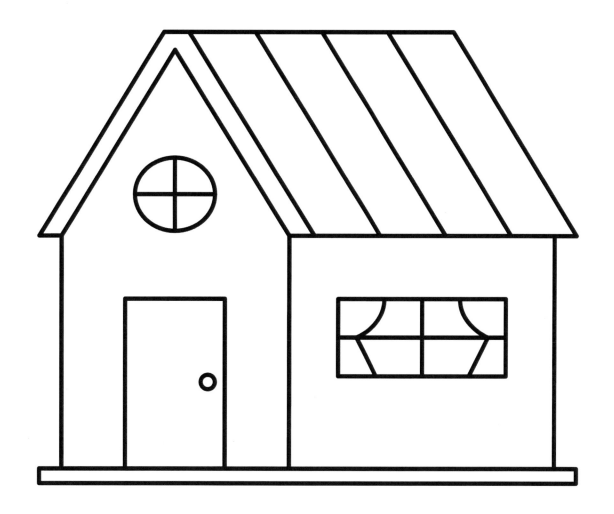

House

منزل

Mango

مانجو

Rose

Orange

البرتقالي

Tree شجرة

This is a camel. There are many stories that mention camels in the Holy Qu'ran, as well as in sayings by the Prophet Muhammad (SAW), which are called hadith.

A male chicken is called a "rooster".
In Arabic, you would called them a:
الديك

These are avocados.
In Arabic, an avocado is called:

أفوكادو

Allah (Subhanahu wa ta'ala) created everything in the world, including the stars and the moon. The word 'Moon' in Arabic is "القمر" (qamar). The Arabic word for 'star' is "نجمة" (najma).

YUMMY EID GOODIES

ا ب ت ث ج

ح خ د ذ ر

ز س ش ص ض

ط ظ ع غ ف

ق ك ل م ن

و ه لا ء ئ

Dates

Did you know that cats are allowed inside of mosques?

Made in United States
North Haven, CT
19 September 2024

57578548R10020